Washington DMV Handbook 2023

Perfect guide for Washington driving test - 2023 edition

Betty Estrada

Copyright © 2023 by Betty Estrada
All rights reserved.

No part of this publication may be reproduced, distributed, or transmitted in any form or by any means, including photocopying, recording, or other electronic or mechanical methods, without the prior written permission of the publisher, except in the case of brief quotations embodied in critical reviews and certain other noncommercial uses permitted by copyright law.

Table of Contents

Chapter 1: Introduction: The Road to Safe and Confident Driving
The Importance of Safe and Responsible Driving
What You Can Expect to Learn
The Purpose of This Handbook

Chapter 2: Getting Started – Your Path to a Washington Driver's License
The Process of Obtaining a Washington Driver's License
Necessary Documents for Your DMV Visit

Chapter 3: Rules of the Road – Navigating Washington's Highways Safely
Understanding Washington's Traffic Laws
Traffic Signals and Signs: Deciphering Their Meanings
Understanding Right-of-Way Rules
Speed Limits: The Need for Caution

Chapter 4: Safe Driving Techniques – Navigating Washington's Roads with Confidence
Defensive Driving: Your Key to Anticipating Hazards
Handling Adverse Weather Conditions
Sharing the Road with Other Vehicles

Chapter 5: Traffic Violations and Penalties - Navigating the Consequences of Breaking the Law

  Common Traffic Violations
  Consequences of Traffic Violations
  Contesting a Traffic Ticket

Chapter 6: Road Signs and Markings - Navigating Washington's Roads with Confidence

  Understanding Road Signs: Categorization and Meanings
  Pavement Markings and Their Meanings
  Quiz: Test Your Road Sign Knowledge

Chapter 7: Parking and Turning - Navigating Washington's Streets with Precision

  Parking Regulations in Washington
  Step-by-Step Guide to Parallel Parking
  Safe Turning Techniques and the Importance of Turn Signals

Chapter 8: Intersections and Lane Usage - Safely Navigating Washington's Crossroads

  Navigating Intersections: Controlled vs. Uncontrolled
  Right-of-Way Rules at Intersections

   Using Lanes Appropriately
   Intersection Safety Tips

Chapter 9: Special Driving Situations – Navigating Unique Challenges with Care

   Driving in School Zones
   Sharing the Road with School Buses
   Navigating Work Zones
   Safely Crossing Railroad Tracks
   Interacting with Pedestrians and Bicyclists

Chapter 10: DUI and Impaired Driving – The Consequences of Driving Under the Influence

   Washington's DUI Laws
   Consequences of DUI Convictions
   Practical Tips for Avoiding Impaired Driving

Chapter 11: Obtaining a Commercial Driver's License (CDL) – Your Path to Becoming a Professional Driver

   Requirements for Obtaining a CDL
   The CDL Written Test
   The CDL Road Test

Chapter 12: Additional Resources – Your Gateway to Success

   Contact Information for DMV and Local Offices
   Online Resources and Practice Tests
   Sample Practice Questions

Index

Chapter 13: Conclusion – Your Journey to Safe and Responsible Driving
Summarizing the Key Points
Encouraging Safe Driving Habits
Best Wishes for Your Success

Appendix: Your Handy Reference
Glossary of Terms
Sample Practice Questions

Chapter 1:

Introduction: The Road to Safe and Confident Driving

Driving is more than just a skill; it's a responsibility that impacts not only your life but also the lives of those sharing the road with you. As you embark on the journey to becoming a licensed driver in Washington State, you are taking on a significant role in ensuring the safety of yourself, your passengers, and fellow road users. Welcome to the "Washington DMV Handbook 2023: Perfect Guide for Washington Driving Test - 2023 Edition."

The Importance of Safe and Responsible Driving

Before we delve into the specifics of passing the Washington driving test, let's take a moment to reflect on the importance of safe and responsible driving. Each year, countless accidents occur on our roads, resulting in injuries, loss of life, and property damage. Many of these accidents are preventable through knowledge, awareness, and adherence to traffic rules. This handbook aims to equip you with the knowledge and skills needed to be a responsible and safe driver, reducing the likelihood of accidents and making our roads safer for everyone.

What You Can Expect to Learn

In the following chapters, we will cover a wide range of topics essential for both new and experienced drivers. Whether you're just starting your journey or seeking a refresher, this book is designed to be your trusted companion. Here's a glimpse of what you can expect to learn:

- How to obtain your Washington driver's license.

- Understanding and following Washington's traffic laws.
- Navigating traffic signals, road signs, and right-of-way rules.
- Practicing safe driving techniques for various road conditions.
- Dealing with traffic violations and their consequences.
- Recognizing and understanding road signs and markings.
- Mastering parking and turning skills.
- Navigating intersections and using lanes effectively.
- Handling special driving situations like school zones, work zones, and railroad crossings.
- Staying informed about DUI laws and avoiding impaired driving.
- Information on obtaining a Commercial Driver's License (CDL).
- Additional resources to aid your preparation.

The Purpose of This Handbook

The primary purpose of this handbook is to serve as a comprehensive and up-to-date guide to help you prepare for the Washington driving test in 2023. Passing this test is a crucial step toward obtaining your driver's license, and we are here to provide you with the knowledge and confidence you need to succeed.

We understand that preparing for a driving test can be both exciting and nerve-wracking, but with the right information and guidance, you can face it with confidence. Our goal is to ensure that you not only pass the test but also become a safe, courteous, and responsible driver who contributes positively to our community.

So, fasten your seatbelt, keep your hands on the wheel, and let's embark on this educational journey together. By the end of this handbook, you'll not only be well-prepared for the Washington driving test but also equipped to make our roads safer for all. Let's get started!

Chapter 2:

Getting Started - Your Path to a Washington Driver's License

Congratulations on taking your first step toward becoming a licensed driver in the beautiful state of Washington! Obtaining a driver's license is a significant milestone, granting you the freedom to explore our scenic landscapes and bustling cities. In this chapter, we'll walk you through the process, eligibility requirements, and the essential documents you'll need when visiting the Department of Motor Vehicles (DMV).

The Process of Obtaining a Washington Driver's License

Obtaining a Washington driver's license involves a series of steps to ensure that you are a responsible and capable driver.

Let's break down the process into simple, easy-to-follow steps:

Step 1: Determine Eligibility

Before you can apply for a Washington driver's license, you need to meet certain eligibility requirements:

Age Requirement: In Washington, you must be at least 16 years old to apply for a standard driver's license. However, there are different age requirements for various types of licenses. For example, you can apply for an instruction permit at the age of 15.

Residency: You must be a Washington resident or provide proof of Washington state residency to be eligible for a Washington driver's license.

Legal Presence: You must be legally present in the United States. If you are not a U.S. citizen, specific documentation is required to establish your legal presence.

Step 2: Prepare for the Knowledge Test
Before you can get behind the wheel, you'll need to pass a knowledge test. This test evaluates your understanding of Washington's traffic laws, road signs, and safe driving practices. To prepare:

- Study the Washington Driver Guide provided by the DMV. It contains all the information you need to know for the test.
- Take advantage of online practice tests and study materials to reinforce your knowledge.
- Schedule an appointment for the knowledge test at your local DMV office.

Step 3: Obtain an Instruction Permit
An instruction permit allows you to practice driving under the supervision of

a licensed adult. Here's what you need to do:

- Visit your local DMV office with the required documents (we'll cover these shortly).
- Pass the knowledge test.
- Pay the appropriate fees.
- Pass a vision screening.
- Submit a completed Parental Authorization Affidavit if you're under 18. This form requires the signature of a parent or legal guardian.

With your instruction permit in hand, you can begin practicing your driving skills, always accompanied by a licensed adult who is at least 21 years old.

Step 4: Gain Practical Experience
To become a skilled and confident driver, you'll need to practice. During this stage:

- Practice driving with your instruction permit.
- Observe all traffic laws, including obeying speed limits and road signs.
- Log your driving hours, as you may be required to provide this information when applying for a full driver's license.

Step 5: Pass the Road Test
When you're ready, schedule an appointment for the road test at your local DMV office. Be prepared to demonstrate your ability to safely operate a vehicle. The examiner will evaluate your skills in various driving situations, such as turning, parking, and merging.

Step 6: Get Your Full Driver's License
Upon passing the road test and meeting all other requirements, you can now obtain your full Washington driver's license. Congratulations, you're now a licensed driver!

Necessary Documents for Your DMV Visit

When you visit the DMV to apply for your Washington driver's license or instruction permit, you'll need to bring specific documents to verify your identity, residency, and legal presence. Here's a list of commonly required documents:

1. Proof of Identity: You'll need to provide a document proving your identity. This can be your birth certificate, passport, or a similar document.

2. Proof of Residency: To demonstrate your Washington residency, bring documents like utility bills, a lease agreement, or a bank statement with your current address.

3. Social Security Number (SSN): If you have an SSN, you'll need to provide your

Social Security card or a document with your SSN on it.

4. Parental Authorization Affidavit: If you're under 18, you'll need this form with your parent or legal guardian's signature.

5. Payment: Be prepared to pay the required fees. The DMV typically accepts cash, checks, or credit/debit cards.

These requirements may vary based on your specific situation, so it's a good idea to check the DMV's website or contact your local DMV office before your visit to ensure you have all the necessary documents.

With this comprehensive guide, you're now well-equipped to begin your journey toward obtaining a Washington driver's license. Take the time to prepare, practice, and familiarize yourself with

Washington's traffic laws, and soon you'll be cruising the scenic roads of the Evergreen State with confidence.

Chapter 3:

Rules of the Road - Navigating Washington's Highways Safely

Welcome to the heart of responsible and safe driving—the understanding and application of traffic laws. In this chapter, we'll delve into Washington's traffic laws, shedding light on key regulations, deciphering the language of traffic signals and signs, clarifying right-of-way rules, and demystifying speed limits for various types of roads. By the end of this chapter, you'll be well-versed in the rules that govern our roadways, helping you become a responsible and law-abiding driver.

Understanding Washington's Traffic Laws

Traffic laws exist to maintain order, ensure safety, and facilitate the smooth flow of traffic. Here, we'll explore some essential aspects of Washington's traffic laws:

1. Obedience to Traffic Control Devices:
- Always obey traffic signals, signs, and pavement markings.
- Follow the instructions of law enforcement officers.

2. Right-of-Way Rules:
- mmmYield the right-of-way to pedestrians in crosswalks.
- Yield to vehicles already in the intersection when you're making a left turn.
- Yield when merging onto a highway or freeway.
- Understand that not all intersections have four-way stops, so be attentive to who has the right-of-way.

3. Turning Rules:

- When turning left at an intersection, yield to oncoming traffic.
- When turning right, yield to pedestrians and bicyclists.

4. Passing and Overtaking:
- Always pass on the left and only when it's safe to do so.
- Do not pass in no-passing zones or on curves.
- Maintain a safe following distance when overtaking other vehicles.

5. *Speed Limits:*
- *Respect posted speed limit*
- *Slow down in school zones, work zones, and residential areas.*
- *Adjust your speed according to road and weather conditions.*

6. Belts and Child Restraints:
- Washington law requires all vehicle occupants to wear seat belts.

- Ensure children are properly secured in age-appropriate child safety seats.

Traffic Signals and Signs: Deciphering Their Meanings

Traffic signals and signs are your guides on the road. Understanding their meanings is crucial for safe driving:

1. Traffic Signals:
- Red Light: Stop. Come to a complete stop before the crosswalk or stop line.
- Green Light: Go if it's safe to do so.
- Yellow Light: Slow down; a red light is imminent.
- Flashing Red Light: Treat as a stop sign.
- Flashing Yellow Light: Proceed with caution; slow down.

2. Road Signs:

- Stop Sign (Octagon): Come to a complete stop.
- Yield Sign (Triangle): Slow down and yield to oncoming traffic.
- Speed Limit Sign (White Rectangle): Indicates the maximum speed allowed in the area.
- No Entry Sign (Red Circle with Line): Entry is prohibited.
- One-Way Sign (White Arrow): Traffic must travel in the direction of the arrow.

Understanding Right-of-Way Rules

Right-of-way rules dictate who proceeds first in specific traffic situations. Let's clarify these rules:

1. Four-Way Stop:
- The vehicle that arrives first or the one to the right goes first.

- If two vehicles arrive simultaneously, the one on the right has the right-of-way.

2. Uncontrolled Intersection:
- Yield to vehicles already in the intersection.

3. Pedestrian Crosswalk:
- Always yield to pedestrians in crosswalks.

4. Merging:
- The vehicle that is merging should yield to traffic already on the highway.

5. Emergency Vehicles:
- Pull over and stop to give the right-of-way to emergency vehicles with lights and sirens activated.

Speed Limits: The Need for Caution

Speed limits are not arbitrary; they are set with safety in mind. Understanding them is vital for responsible driving:

1. Residential Areas:
- Speed limits in residential areas are typically 25 mph unless posted otherwise.

2. School Zones:
- Speed limits in school zones are often 20 mph when children are present.

3. Highways and Freeways:
- Speed limits on highways and freeways can vary but are usually between 60 and 70 mph.

4. Work Zones:
- Reduced speed limits are enforced in work zones for the safety of workers and drivers.

5. **Special Zones:**
   - Always pay attention to speed limit signs in construction zones, curves, and other special areas.

Navigating Washington's roadways safely and responsibly is a shared responsibility. By understanding and adhering to traffic laws, signals, signs, right-of-way rules, and speed limits, you contribute to a safer and more enjoyable driving experience for all. Always stay informed about current laws and regulations, and remember that safe driving is not just about following the rules; it's about being considerate and alert on the road. In the chapters that follow, we will continue to explore essential aspects of safe and responsible driving, equipping you with the knowledge and skills to become a confident and law-abiding driver.

Chapter 4:

Safe Driving Techniques - Navigating Washington's Roads with Confidence

Safe driving isn't just about knowing the rules of the road; it's also about mastering techniques that protect you and those around you. In this chapter, we'll delve into safe driving techniques that every driver should be well-versed in. From defensive driving strategies to handling adverse weather conditions and sharing the road harmoniously with various vehicles, you'll gain the skills and knowledge needed to drive confidently and responsibly.

Defensive Driving: Your Key to Anticipating Hazards

Defensive driving is a proactive approach to road safety. It involves staying alert, being aware of your surroundings, and anticipating potential hazards. Here's how you can become a defensive driver:

1. Stay Alert:
- Pay full attention to the road. Avoid distractions like texting or using your phone.
- Be aware of the traffic around you, including the actions of other drivers.

2. Maintain a Safe Following Distance:
- Keep a safe following distance from the vehicle in front of you. A general rule is the "three-second rule." Choose a fixed point, and when the car ahead passes it, count "one thousand one, one thousand two, one thousand three." If you reach that point before you finish counting, you're following too closely.

3. Watch for Signs of Aggressive Drivers:
- Be cautious around aggressive drivers who may exhibit behaviors like tailgating, weaving in and out of traffic, or excessive speeding.
- Avoid engaging with aggressive drivers; instead, let them pass safely.

4. Plan for the Unexpected:
- Anticipate the actions of other drivers and be prepared for sudden stops or lane changes.
- Scan the road ahead for potential hazards, such as stopped vehicles or pedestrians.

Handling Adverse Weather Conditions

Washington's climate can bring various weather challenges, from heavy rain to snow and fog. Here's how to navigate adverse conditions safely:

1. **Rain:**
   - Reduce your speed during rain showers to prevent hydroplaning.
   - Ensure your windshield wipers are in good condition for optimal visibility.

2. **Snow and Ice:**
   - Equip your vehicle with appropriate tires or chains for snowy and icy conditions.
   - Drive at a reduced speed and increase your following distance.

3. **Fog:**
   - Use low-beam headlights or fog lights to improve visibility in foggy conditions.
   - Reduce your speed and avoid sudden maneuvers.

Sharing the Road with Other Vehicles

Sharing the road with a variety of vehicles, from motorcycles to large trucks, requires cooperation and awareness. Here's how to do it safely:

1. Motorcycles:
- Give motorcyclists a full lane width. They have the same rights as other vehicles.
- Be vigilant for motorcycles in your blind spots.

2. Large Trucks and Buses:
- Avoid driving in a large truck's blind spots, especially directly behind or alongside them.
- Give extra space when passing trucks or buses, as they may have larger blind spots.

3. Bicycles:

- Always yield the right-of-way to bicyclists at intersections and crosswalks.
- Maintain a safe distance when passing bicyclists and be aware of bike lanes.

4. **Emergency Vehicles:**
   - When you see or hear emergency vehicles with lights and sirens, pull over to the right and stop to allow them to pass.

5. **Pedestrians:**
   - Yield the right-of-way to pedestrians in crosswalks.
   - Be extra cautious in areas with heavy foot traffic, such as school zones and downtown areas.

Safe driving techniques are not just a set of skills; they are a mindset that prioritizes the well-being of all road users. By adopting defensive driving strategies, knowing how to handle adverse weather conditions, and being considerate when sharing the road with other vehicles, you contribute to a safer and more harmonious driving environment in Washington.

Safety on the road is a shared responsibility. Be patient, stay alert, and always follow the rules of the road. By doing so, you not only protect yourself and your passengers but also contribute to the collective effort of making Washington's roads safer for everyone. In the following chapters, we will explore more aspects of responsible and confident driving, helping you become a skilled and courteous driver.

Chapter 5:

Traffic Violations and Penalties - Navigating the Consequences of Breaking the Law

Traffic violations are not just rule infractions; they can have significant consequences. In this chapter, we'll explore common traffic violations that you should avoid, understand the penalties for these violations, including fines, points on your license, and possible license suspension, and learn how to contest a traffic ticket if you believe it was unjustly issued. By the end of this chapter, you'll be well-informed about the repercussions of breaking traffic laws and how to navigate them responsibly.

Common Traffic Violations

Traffic violations can vary in severity, but all are essential to be aware of. Here are some common ones:

1. Speeding:
- Exceeding the posted speed limit is one of the most frequent traffic violations.
- Speed limits are there for safety, and exceeding them endangers everyone on the road.

2. Running Red Lights and Stop Signs:
- Failing to stop at a red light or stop sign is dangerous and a violation of traffic laws.
- These violations can lead to severe accidents and injuries.

3. Reckless Driving:
- Reckless driving includes aggressive behaviors like tailgating, excessive

speeding, and weaving through traffic.
- It endangers both the driver and others on the road.

4. Driving Under the Influence (DUI):
- DUI is a serious offense and involves operating a vehicle while impaired by alcohol or drugs.
- The legal limit for blood alcohol concentration (BAC) in Washington is 0.08%.

5. Distracted Driving:
- Using a mobile phone or engaging in other distracting activities while driving is illegal.
- It diverts your attention from the road and increases the risk of accidents.

6. Failure to Yield:

- Not yielding the right-of-way when required, such as at pedestrian crosswalks, is a common violation.
- It can lead to accidents involving pedestrians and other vehicles.

Consequences of Traffic Violations

Traffic violations come with consequences that can affect your driving record, finances, and even your ability to drive legally. Here's what you can expect:

1. Fines:
- Most traffic violations result in fines that you'll need to pay.
- The amount of the fine varies depending on the violation's severity.

2. Points on Your License:
- Many violations lead to points being added to your driving record.

- Accumulating too many points can lead to increased insurance costs and even license suspension.

3. License Suspension:
- Certain violations, such as repeated DUI offenses or excessive speeding, can result in a suspended or revoked license.
- You may be required to attend traffic school or meet other conditions to reinstate your license.

4. Increased Insurance Costs:
- A poor driving record with multiple violations can lead to higher insurance premiums.

Contesting a Traffic Ticket

If you believe you've received a traffic ticket unfairly, you have the right to contest it. Here's how to do so:

1. Review the Ticket:
- Carefully read the ticket to understand the specific violation you're being charged with and the details of the incident.

2. Gather Evidence:
- Collect any evidence that supports your case. This might include photographs, witness statements, or documentation.

3. Request a Hearing:
- Contact the court indicated on the ticket and request a hearing to contest the violation.

4. Prepare for the Hearing:
- Before the hearing, organize your evidence and be prepared to present your case.

5. Attend the Hearing:

- Attend the scheduled hearing and present your case to the judge.

6. Follow the Judge's Decision:
- The judge will make a decision based on the evidence presented.
- If your ticket is dismissed, you won't face penalties. If it's upheld, you'll be responsible for the associated fines and consequences.

Understanding traffic violations, their consequences, and your rights when contesting a ticket is crucial for responsible and informed driving. While it's always best to obey traffic laws to avoid violations, accidents, and penalties, knowing how to navigate the legal process when faced with a ticket is also essential.

Safe and responsible driving is not only about avoiding penalties but also about ensuring the safety of yourself and others on the road. In the following chapters, we will continue to explore essential aspects of safe and responsible driving in Washington.

Chapter 6:

Road Signs and Markings - Navigating Washington's Roads with Confidence

Road signs and markings are like a silent language that communicates important information to drivers. In this chapter, we'll categorize and explain various road signs, including regulatory, warning, and informational signs. We'll also delve into pavement markings and their meanings. To help reinforce your knowledge, we've included a quiz at the end of the chapter to practice recognizing road signs. By the end, you'll be well-prepared to interpret the messages conveyed by these critical elements of road safety.

Understanding Road Signs: Categorization and Meanings

Road signs are categorized into three main types: regulatory, warning, and informational. Let's explore each category and their meanings:

1. Regulatory Signs:

- Stop Sign (Octagon): You must come to a complete stop at this sign.
- Yield Sign (Triangle): Slow down and yield to other traffic.
- Speed Limit Sign (White Rectangle): Indicates the maximum speed allowed in the area.
- No Entry Sign (Red Circle with Line): Entry is prohibited.
- One-Way Sign (White Arrow): Traffic must travel in the direction of the arrow.

2. Warning Signs:

- School Zone Sign (Yellow Pentagon): Indicates a school zone. Watch for children and obey reduced speed limits.
- Curve Sign (Black Arrow): The road ahead curves in the direction of the arrow.
- Deer Crossing Sign (Yellow Diamond): Caution, deer may cross the road.
- Railroad Crossing Sign (Round Yellow Sign with X): Prepare to stop for a train crossing.
- Slippery When Wet Sign (Yellow Diamond): The road may be slippery when wet. Drive with caution.

3. Informational Signs:

- Route Sign (Various Shapes): Indicates the route number.
- Hospital Sign (White H on Blue Background): Shows the way to a nearby hospital.

- Rest Area Sign (Blue Pillow on White Background): Indicates the location of a rest area.
- Gas Station Sign (Blue Sign with Gas Pump): Shows the way to a gas station.
- Exit Sign (Green Sign with Arrow): Marks the exit from a highway.

Pavement Markings and Their Meanings

Pavement markings are painted lines and symbols on the road surface that convey important information. Here's what they mean:

1. Solid Yellow Line:
- Indicates a no-passing zone. Do not cross the line to pass other vehicles.

2. Broken Yellow Line:
- Allows passing when safe and legal to do so.

3. **Solid White Line:**
    - Marks the right edge of the roadway or separates lanes of traffic moving in the same direction.
    - Do not cross a solid white line unless necessary.

4. **Broken White Line:**
    - Separates lanes of traffic moving in the same direction.
    - You may change lanes when it is safe to do so.

5. **Solid Double Yellow Line:**
    - Indicates a no-passing zone on both sides.
    - Crossing is prohibited.

6. **Solid White Line with Arrows:**
    - Indicates a reversible lane. Pay attention to the direction of the arrows to know which way you can travel.

7. Crosswalk Markings:
- White lines on the road indicate pedestrian crosswalks.
- Stop for pedestrians at crosswalks.

8. Stop Line:
- A solid white line across your lane at an intersection indicates where you must stop when facing a red light or stop sign.

9. Bicycle Lane Markings:
- White lines and symbols on the road designate bicycle lanes.
- Do not drive in bicycle lanes except when turning or parking.

Quiz: Test Your Road Sign Knowledge

Let's put your road sign knowledge to the test. Can you identify the following road signs?

1. Which sign indicates a school zone?
   - A) Stop Sign
   - B) Yellow Diamond with a Deer
   - C) Yellow Pentagon

2. What does a solid double yellow line indicate?
   - A) No-passing zone on both sides
   - B) Passing allowed
   - C) Reversible lane

3. Which sign marks the exit from a highway?
   - A) Blue Pillow on White Background
   - B) Round Yellow Sign with X
   - C) White H on Blue Background

4. What does a solid white line on the road typically indicate?
   - A) No-passing zone
   - B) Passing allowed
   - C) Bicycle lane

5. What should you do when you see a crosswalk marking on the road?
- A) Speed up to clear the area quickly
- B) Stop for pedestrians if they are in or approaching the crosswalk
- C) Honk your horn to alert pedestrians

Answers:
1. C) Yellow Pentagon
2. A) No-passing zone on both sides
3. A) Blue Pillow on White Background
4. A) No-passing zone
5. B) Stop for pedestrians if they are in or approaching the crosswalk

Understanding road signs and pavement markings is essential for safe and responsible driving. By categorizing and interpreting various signs and knowing the meanings of pavement markings, you can navigate Washington's roads with confidence. Remember that these signs and markings are there to keep you and other road users safe. In the following chapters, we will continue to explore important aspects of responsible driving in Washington.

Chapter 7:

Parking and Turning - Navigating Washington's Streets with Precision

Parking and turning are essential aspects of responsible driving. In this chapter, we'll delve into Washington's parking regulations, including parallel parking, handicapped parking, and time limits. You'll also find step-by-step instructions for parallel parking, guidance on safe turning techniques, and an emphasis on the importance of using turn signals. By the end of this chapter, you'll be equipped with the skills and knowledge to park and turn with precision and safety.

Parking Regulations in Washington

Parking regulations are in place to ensure that parking is orderly and accessible to all. Familiarize yourself with these rules to avoid fines and inconveniences:

1. Parallel Parking:
- When parallel parking on the right side of the road, your vehicle's right wheels should be within 12 inches of the curb.
- When parallel parking on the left side of the road, your vehicle's left wheels should be within 12 inches of the curb.

2. Handicap Parking:
- Handicapped parking spaces are reserved for individuals with disabilities. Using these spaces without a valid handicap permit is illegal and subject to fines.
- The penalty for parking in a handicapped space without proper authorization can be significant.

3. Time Limits:

- Pay attention to posted time limits for parking in specific areas. Overstaying these limits may result in fines or towing.

4. **No-Parking Zones:**
   - Respect no-parking zones, which are marked by red curbs, signs, or road markings.
   - Parking in a no-parking zone can lead to fines and towing.

5. **Fire Hydrants:**
   - Do not park within 15 feet of a fire hydrant. This ensures access to emergency vehicles.

Step-by-Step Guide to Parallel Parking

Parallel parking can be challenging, but with practice and the right technique, you can master it. Here's a step-by-step guide:

1. **Find a Suitable Space:**
   - Identify a parking space that is at least 1.5 times the length of your vehicle.

2. **Signal and Position:**
   - Signal your intention to park and pull up alongside the vehicle in front of the space.
   - Align your rear bumper with the rear bumper of the parked vehicle.

3. **Check Blind Spots:**
   - Look over your shoulder and check your blind spots to ensure it's safe to proceed.

4. **Begin the Maneuver:**
   - Turn the steering wheel fully to the right (for right-side parking) or fully to the left (for left-side parking).

5. Reverse Slowly:
- Start reversing slowly, keeping an eye on the curb and the vehicle behind you.

6. Straighten the Wheels:
- When your front seat lines up with the rear bumper of the parked vehicle, straighten your wheels.

7. Continue Reversing:
- Keep reversing until your vehicle is parallel to the curb and your wheels are within 12 inches of it.

8. Adjust as Needed:
- Make any necessary adjustments to ensure you are properly aligned with the curb.

9. Signal and Secure:
- Signal that you're pulling away from the curb and move forward to center your vehicle in the parking space.

Safe Turning Techniques and the Importance of Turn Signals

Safe turning is fundamental to avoiding accidents and ensuring a smooth flow of traffic. Here are some essential turning techniques:

1. Use Turn Signals:
- Always use your turn signals to indicate your intention to turn or change lanes.
- Signal at least 100 feet before your turn.

2. Check Blind Spots:
- Before turning or changing lanes, check your blind spots by looking over your shoulder.

3. Right Turns:
- When making a right turn, stay in the right lane.

- Yield the right-of-way to pedestrians and other vehicles.

4. Left Turns:
- When making a left turn, stay in the left lane or the lane closest to the centerline.
- Yield the right-of-way to oncoming traffic.

5. U-Turns:
- U-turns are not allowed in some areas, so pay attention to signs and regulations.
- Only make a U-turn when it's safe and legal to do so.

6. Roundabouts:
- Yield to vehicles already in the roundabout.
- Enter the roundabout when there is a safe gap in traffic.

7. Check for Pedestrians and Bicyclists:

- Be especially vigilant for pedestrians and bicyclists when turning.
- Always yield to them in crosswalks and bike lanes.

Parking and turning are everyday driving maneuvers that require precision and adherence to rules. By understanding Washington's parking regulations, mastering parallel parking, and practicing safe turning techniques, you contribute to safer roads and a more organized flow of traffic.

Using turn signals is not just a courtesy; it's a legal requirement. Proper signaling and turning techniques help prevent accidents and ensure the safety of all road users. In the following chapters, we will continue to explore essential aspects of responsible driving in Washington.

Chapter 8:

Intersections and Lane Usage - Safely Navigating Washington's Crossroads

Intersections are the crossroads of our roadways, where paths converge and decisions must be made. In this chapter, we'll provide comprehensive guidance on navigating intersections, whether they are controlled or uncontrolled. We'll clarify right-of-way rules in different scenarios and explain how to use lanes appropriately, including turning lanes and HOV (High-Occupancy Vehicle) lanes. By the end of this chapter, you'll have the knowledge and skills to approach intersections with confidence and make informed decisions on lane usage.

Navigating Intersections: Controlled vs. Uncontrolled

Intersections come in two main types: controlled and uncontrolled. Understanding how to approach each is crucial for safe driving:

1. Controlled Intersections:

- Traffic Signals: At intersections with traffic signals, obey the signals' indications.
- Stop Signs: At intersections with stop signs, come to a complete stop and yield to cross traffic before proceeding.

2. Uncontrolled Intersections:

- At uncontrolled intersections (those without signals or signs), yield to any vehicle that arrives at the intersection before you.

- When vehicles arrive simultaneously, the vehicle on the right has the right-of-way.

Right-of-Way Rules at Intersections

Right-of-way rules dictate who has priority at intersections and ensure safe and orderly traffic flow. Here's a breakdown of right-of-way rules in various scenarios:

1. Four-Way Stops:

- At a four-way stop, the vehicle that arrives first or the one to the right goes first.
- If two vehicles arrive simultaneously, the one on the right has the right-of-way.

2. Uncontrolled Intersections:

- Yield to vehicles that reach the intersection before you.

3. Turning Left:

- When turning left at an intersection without signals, yield to oncoming traffic.
- If you have a green left-turn arrow, you have the right-of-way.

4. Pedestrian Crosswalks:

- Always yield to pedestrians in crosswalks.
- Wait until the crosswalk is clear before proceeding.

Using Lanes Appropriately

Lanes on the road serve specific purposes and must be used correctly. Here's how to use them appropriately:

1. Turning Lanes:

- Use designated turning lanes when turning left or right.
- Signal your intention to turn and merge into the appropriate turning lane.

2. HOV (High-Occupancy Vehicle) Lanes:

- HOV lanes are reserved for vehicles with a minimum number of occupants (usually two or more).
- Observe posted signs and requirements for HOV lane usage.

3. Merge Lanes:

- Merge lanes are used to enter or exit the main flow of traffic.
- Signal your intent to merge, check blind spots, and merge smoothly.

4. Passing Lanes:

- Passing lanes are used to overtake slower-moving vehicles.
- Return to the right lane once you have passed the slower vehicle.

5. Bicycle Lanes:

- Bicycle lanes are reserved for bicyclists.
- Do not drive or park in bicycle lanes except when turning or parking where permitted.

6. Bus Lanes:

- Bus lanes are reserved for buses.
- Do not drive in bus lanes unless you are a bus or authorized vehicle.

7. Shoulder Lanes:

- The shoulder lane is not intended for regular travel.

- Use the shoulder only in emergencies, such as a breakdown.

Intersection Safety Tips

Safety at intersections is a top priority. Here are some additional tips to enhance your intersection navigation:

1. Approach with Caution:
- Reduce speed when approaching an intersection, especially if it's unclear who has the right-of-way.
- Scan for pedestrians, bicyclists, and other vehicles.

2. Look Left-Right-Left:
- Before proceeding at a stop sign or uncontrolled intersection, look left, then right, and left again to ensure it's safe to proceed.

3. Maintain a Safe Following Distance:

- Keep a safe distance from the vehicle in front of you to allow for sudden stops.

4. Be Predictable:
- Use turn signals to indicate your intentions to other drivers.

5. Avoid Distractions:
- Avoid distractions like texting or adjusting the radio when approaching and navigating intersections.

Intersections are dynamic spaces where traffic paths intersect, making them both critical and potentially hazardous. By understanding the differences between controlled and uncontrolled intersections, knowing right-of-way rules, and using lanes appropriately, you can navigate these crossroads with precision and safety.

Always prioritize safety, especially at intersections, where the risk of accidents is higher. Respect right-of-way rules, use lanes correctly, and be a predictable and attentive driver. In the following chapters, we will continue to explore essential aspects of responsible driving in Washington.

Chapter 9:

Special Driving Situations - Navigating Unique Challenges with Care

As a responsible driver, you'll encounter various special driving situations that require extra attention and care. In this chapter, we'll discuss driving in school zones, sharing the road with school buses, obeying school bus stop signs, navigating work zones, crossing railroad tracks safely, and interacting with pedestrians and bicyclists. By understanding and following the rules for these situations, you'll contribute to safer roads and better experiences for all road users.

Driving in School Zones

School zones are areas near schools where traffic rules are strictly enforced to protect children. Here's what you need to know:

1. Reduced Speed Limits:
- Be prepared to reduce your speed in school zones, often indicated by flashing lights and reduced speed limit signs.
- Always obey the posted speed limit, which is typically lower during school hours.

2. Watch for Pedestrians:
- Be vigilant for children crossing the street, especially near crosswalks and school entrances.
- Stop for pedestrians in crosswalks and school crossings.

3. No Passing:
- Passing other vehicles in a school zone is generally prohibited.

Sharing the Road with School Buses

School buses transport precious cargo—children. Here's how to safely share the road with school buses:

1. Stop for School Buses:
- When a school bus stops and activates its flashing red lights, you must stop as well, regardless of the direction of travel.
- Wait until the bus deactivates its lights and the driver signals that it's safe to proceed.

2. No Passing:
- Never pass a school bus that is loading or unloading children.
- Passing a stopped school bus is illegal and dangerous.

3. Watch for Children:
- Be extra cautious when near school buses, as children may enter or exit the bus unexpectedly.

Navigating Work Zones

Work zones are areas where road construction or maintenance is taking place. Follow these guidelines for safe navigation:

1. Reduced Speed Limits:
- Observe reduced speed limits posted in work zones.
- Slower speeds are necessary to protect both workers and drivers.

2. Follow Signs and Flaggers:
- Pay close attention to signs, cones, and flaggers directing traffic through the work zone.
- Follow their instructions carefully.

3. Merge Promptly:
- Merge as soon as possible when lanes are closed in a work zone.
- Avoid last-minute lane changes.

Safely Crossing Railroad Tracks

Crossing railroad tracks requires caution to avoid accidents. Here's how to do it safely:

1. Stop for Trains:
- Always stop when the railroad crossing gates are down, or red lights are flashing.
- Wait until the train has passed, and the gates or lights indicate it's safe to proceed.

2. Leave Room for Buses and Trucks:
- When waiting at a railroad crossing, leave enough space for buses and trucks to clear the tracks.

3. Look and Listen:
- Even if there are no gates or lights, look both ways and listen for approaching trains before crossing.

Interacting with Pedestrians and Bicyclists

Pedestrians and bicyclists share the road with motor vehicles. Here's how to interact safely:

1. Yield to Pedestrians:
- Always yield the right-of-way to pedestrians in crosswalks and at intersections.
- Be patient and allow them to cross safely.

2. Keep a Safe Distance:
- When passing bicyclists, leave at least three feet of space between your vehicle and the cyclist.
- Do not follow closely behind bicyclists.

3. Be Patient:

- Bicyclists may ride slower than motor vehicles. Be patient when driving behind them.
- Do not honk your horn unnecessarily.

4. Watch for Turning Bicyclists:
- Bicyclists may make unexpected turns or movements. Be aware and cautious around them.

Special driving situations require careful attention and adherence to specific rules. By understanding how to drive safely in school zones, share the road with school buses, navigate work zones, cross railroad tracks safely, and interact respectfully with pedestrians and bicyclists, you contribute to a safer and more harmonious road environment.

Special situations involve vulnerable road users, such as children and pedestrians. Prioritize their safety and follow the rules to ensure everyone reaches their destination safely. In the following chapters, we will continue to explore essential aspects of responsible driving in Washington.

Chapter 10:

DUI and Impaired Driving - The Consequences of Driving Under the Influence

Driving under the influence (DUI) poses a serious threat to road safety. In this chapter, we'll explain Washington's laws regarding DUI, including blood alcohol concentration (BAC) limits. We'll also detail the severe consequences of DUI convictions, such as fines, license suspension, and mandatory alcohol education programs. Additionally, we'll offer practical tips for avoiding impaired driving situations. By the end of this chapter, you'll understand the gravity of impaired driving and how to prevent it.

Washington's DUI Laws

Washington state has stringent laws to deter and penalize DUI offenses. Understanding these laws is crucial:

1. Blood Alcohol Concentration (BAC) Limits:
- The legal limit for BAC in Washington is 0.08%. If your BAC is at or above this limit, you can be charged with DUI.

2. Zero Tolerance for Minors:
- For drivers under 21, Washington has a zero-tolerance policy. Any detectable BAC above 0.00% can result in penalties.

3. Marijuana and Other Drugs:
- DUI laws also apply to driving under the influence of marijuana and other drugs.

- Officers can conduct field sobriety tests if they suspect drug impairment.

Consequences of DUI Convictions

DUI convictions in Washington lead to severe consequences that affect your life and driving privileges:

1. Fines:
- DUI convictions result in substantial fines that can strain your finances.

2. License Suspension:
- Your driver's license may be suspended for a period determined by the court.
- A first-time DUI offense can result in a 90-day license suspension.

3. Mandatory Alcohol Education:

- DUI offenders are often required to complete alcohol education programs at their own expense.

4. **Ignition Interlock Device (IID):**
   - For some DUI offenses, you may be required to install an IID in your vehicle, which requires you to pass a breathalyzer test before starting the car.

5. **Probation:**
   - DUI offenders may be placed on probation, with conditions such as regular check-ins with a probation officer.

6. **Criminal Record:**
   - A DUI conviction can lead to a permanent criminal record that may affect future employment opportunities.

7. **Increased Insurance Costs:**

- Your auto insurance rates will likely increase significantly after a DUI conviction.

Practical Tips for Avoiding Impaired Driving

Avoiding impaired driving is crucial for your safety and the safety of others. Here are practical tips to help you stay responsible:

1. Plan Ahead:
- Always plan for a sober ride home if you anticipate drinking alcohol or using drugs.
- Designate a sober driver or arrange for a taxi, rideshare service, or public transportation.

2. Use Mobile Apps:
- There are various mobile apps that can help you find a sober ride or

provide information about local transportation options.

3. Monitor Medications:
- Be aware of the potential side effects of prescription or over-the-counter medications.
- Consult your healthcare provider to ensure they won't impair your driving.

4. Host Responsibly:
- If you're hosting a gathering where alcohol is served, ensure that guests have a safe way to get home.
- Don't let anyone leave your home if they're impaired.

5. Educate Yourself:
- Learn about the effects of alcohol and drugs on your ability to drive.
- Understanding the risks can deter impaired driving.

6. Be a Responsible Passenger:
- If someone you know is impaired and intends to drive, take their keys and help them find an alternative way home.

7. Know the Consequences:
- Familiarize yourself with the consequences of DUI convictions in Washington to make informed decisions.

Driving under the influence of alcohol or drugs is not only illegal but also life-threatening. Washington's DUI laws are strict, and the consequences of DUI convictions are severe. By understanding these laws, recognizing the potential consequences, and following practical tips to avoid impaired driving situations, you can make responsible choices on the road.

Choosing not to drive under the influence isn't just a legal requirement; it's a moral obligation to protect yourself and others from harm. In the following chapters, we will continue to explore essential aspects of responsible driving in Washington.

Chapter 11:

Obtaining a Commercial Driver's License (CDL) - Your Path to Becoming a Professional Driver

A Commercial Driver's License (CDL) opens doors to exciting career opportunities in the world of professional driving. In this chapter, we'll outline the requirements for obtaining a CDL, explain the CDL written test, and describe the CDL road test. Whether you're considering a career as a truck driver or bus operator, understanding the CDL process in Washington is your key to success.

Requirements for Obtaining a CDL

Before you embark on your journey to obtaining a CDL, it's essential to meet specific requirements:

1. **Age Requirement:**
   - To apply for a CDL in Washington, you must be at least 18 years old for intrastate (within the state) driving or 21 years old for interstate (crossing state lines) driving.

2. **Medical Qualifications:**
   - You must pass a medical examination conducted by a certified medical examiner listed on the Federal Motor Carrier Safety Administration (FMCSA) National Registry.
   - The medical exam assesses your physical fitness to operate a commercial vehicle safely.

3. **Background Checks:**
   - CDL applicants undergo background checks, including criminal history and driving record checks.

- Certain criminal convictions may disqualify you from obtaining a CDL.

4. **Knowledge Test:**
   - Pass the CDL knowledge test, which assesses your understanding of the rules and regulations governing commercial driving.

The CDL Written Test

The CDL written test is a critical step in the CDL application process. It evaluates your knowledge of essential topics related to commercial driving. Here's an overview of the topics covered:

1. **General Knowledge:**
   - Covers basic driving safety rules, vehicle inspections, and the effects of alcohol and drugs on driving.

2. **Transporting Cargo Safely:**

- Focuses on securing cargo, weight distribution, and handling hazardous materials.

3. Air Brakes:
- Addresses the operation and maintenance of vehicles equipped with air brake systems.

4. Combination Vehicles:
- Pertains to driving combination vehicles, such as tractor-trailers.

5. Doubles/Triples:
- Covers the operation of double and triple trailers.

6. Tank Vehicles:
- Focuses on safe operation and handling of tank vehicles.

7. HazMat (Hazardous Materials):

- Addresses the transportation of hazardous materials, including placarding and emergency response.

8. Passenger Vehicles:
- Pertains to the safe operation of passenger-carrying vehicles like buses.

9. School Buses:
- Covers the specific rules and requirements for driving school buses.

10. Pre-Trip Vehicle Inspection:
- Evaluate your ability to inspect a commercial vehicle for safety before a trip.

The CDL Road Test

Once you've successfully passed the CDL written test and obtained a commercial learner's permit (CLP), you're eligible to take the CDL road test. Here's what you can expect during this practical examination:

1. Vehicle Inspection:
- You'll be asked to perform a thorough pre-trip vehicle inspection to ensure the vehicle is safe to operate.

2. Basic Controls:
- Demonstrate your ability to control the commercial vehicle through maneuvers such as backing, turning, and parking.

3. On-Road Driving:
- Take to the road with an examiner to showcase your driving skills.
- Follow traffic laws, make proper lane changes, and respond to various driving scenarios.

4. Specific Skills Test:

- Depending on the type of CDL you're pursuing (e.g., Class A, B, or C), you may be required to perform additional skills tests related to the specific type of vehicle you'll operate.

Obtaining a Commercial Driver's License (CDL) is a significant achievement that can lead to a rewarding career in professional driving. By meeting the necessary requirements, passing the CDL written test, and successfully completing the CDL road test, you can embark on your journey as a qualified commercial driver.

Commercial driving comes with significant responsibilities and the need for ongoing safety and professionalism. As you continue your journey in the world of professional driving, always prioritize safety, adhere to regulations, and stay up-to-date with industry standards and practices.

Chapter 12:

Additional Resources - Your Gateway to Success

In your journey to becoming a safe and responsible driver, having access to reliable resources is key. This chapter provides you with valuable information, including contact details for the DMV and local DMV offices, online resources for practice tests and study materials, sample practice questions to enhance your preparation, and an index for easy navigation within this book. Let's explore these resources that will support you on your path to success.

Contact Information for DMV and Local Offices

It's essential to know where to reach out for official information and assistance. Here are the contact details for the Department of Motor Vehicles (DMV) and local DMV offices in Washington:

Washington Department of Licensing (DOL):

- Website: [Washington DOL](https://www.dol.wa.gov/)
- Phone: 360-902-3900

Local DMV Offices:

- For the address and contact information of the nearest local DMV office, visit the official DOL website or call the central phone number provided above.

Online Resources and Practice Tests

Studying for your driver's license or CDL exam has never been easier, thanks to a wealth of online resources. Here are some recommended websites where you can access practice tests and additional study materials:

1. [Washington DOL Practice Tests](https://www.dmv-written-test.com/washington/practice-test-1.html):
    - This website offers free practice tests for various types of licenses, allowing you to assess your knowledge and boost your confidence.

2. [Driving-Tests.org](https://driving-tests.org/washington/):
    - Driving-Tests.org provides a variety of practice tests and resources specifically tailored to Washington state's driving exams.

3. [CDL Practice Test](https://cdlpracticetest.com/):
   - If you're preparing for your Commercial Driver's License (CDL) exam, this website offers free practice tests categorized by CDL class and endorsements.

Sample Practice Questions

To help you get a feel for the types of questions you might encounter on your written test, here are some sample practice questions:

1. General Knowledge:
   - Question: What should you do if you are approaching a traffic signal displaying a steady yellow light?
   - Answer: Slow down and prepare to stop.

2. Road Signs:

- Question: What does a red octagonal sign mean?
- Answer: Stop.

3. **Safe Driving Practices:**
   - Question: When is it appropriate to use your vehicle's horn?
   - Answer: To alert other drivers of your presence when necessary, such as to avoid a collision.

4. **CDL Specific (Air Brakes):**
   - Question: What does the air brake system do?
   - Answer: Uses compressed air to operate the vehicle's brakes.

Index

To help you quickly locate specific information within this book, here's an index of topics covered:

- A: Age Requirements (Page 12)

- B: Blind Spots (Page 32)
- C: CDL Written Test (Page 86)
- D: Defensive Driving (Page 102)
- E: Emergency Vehicles (Page 24)
- F: Fire Hydrants (Page 54)
- G: General Knowledge (Page 88)
- H: Hazardous Materials (Page 109)
- I: Intersections (Page 102)
- J: Judge's Decision (Page 41)
- K: Lane Usage (Page 101)
- L: Lane Changes (Page 30)
- M: Merging (Page 15)
- N: Navigating Work Zones (Page 72)
- O: Obtaining a Driver's License (Page 100)
- P: Parking (Page 101)
- Q: Questions (Sample Practice) (Page 110)
- R: Road Signs (Page 43)
- S: Special Driving Situations (Page 58)
- T: Turning (Page 101)
- U: U-Turns (Page 58)
- V: Vehicle Inspections (Page 100)

- W: Work Zones (Page 101)
- X: (N/A)
- Y: (N/A)
- Z: (N/A)

Armed with this wealth of resources, you're well-prepared to embark on your journey to becoming a safe and responsible driver. Whether you're studying for your learner's permit, driver's license, or Commercial Driver's License (CDL), these resources will enhance your knowledge and boost your confidence.

Learning to drive is a journey, and every step you take brings you closer to your destination. Stay focused, stay safe, and enjoy the freedom and responsibility that come with being a licensed driver. Best of luck with your exams and happy driving!

Chapter 13:

Conclusion - Your Journey to Safe and Responsible Driving

Congratulations on reaching the conclusion of this comprehensive guide on safe and responsible driving in Washington! Throughout this book, we've covered a wide range of topics to help you prepare for the Washington driving test and become a skilled, responsible driver. Let's take a moment to summarize the key points covered, encourage you to continue studying and practicing safe driving habits, and express our best wishes for your success on the Washington driving test.

Summarizing the Key Points

In your journey to becoming a safe and responsible driver, you've learned valuable information, including:

1. Obtaining a Driver's License: We discussed the steps to obtain your learner's permit and driver's license, including the written and road tests.

2. Vehicle Inspections: You've learned the importance of inspecting your vehicle before each trip to ensure it's safe to drive.

3. Road Signs: We covered the various types of road signs and their meanings to help you navigate the road safely.

4. Safe Driving Practices: Defensive driving techniques, such as maintaining a safe following distance and scanning for potential hazards, were highlighted.

5. Traffic Violations and Penalties: Understanding common traffic violations and their consequences is crucial for responsible driving.

6. Road Signs and Markings: Categorizing and explaining road signs and pavement markings to enhance your road awareness.

7. Parking and Turning: Detailed instructions for parking, parallel parking, and safe turning techniques were provided.

8. Intersections and Lane Usage: Comprehensive guidance on navigating intersections and using lanes appropriately.

9. Special Driving Situations: Tips for driving in school zones, work zones, near railroad tracks, and interacting with pedestrians and bicyclists were discussed.

10. DUI and Impaired Driving: The severe consequences of driving under the influence of alcohol or drugs and practical tips for avoiding impaired driving were covered.

11. Obtaining a CDL: Requirements, the CDL written test and the CDL road test were outlined for those pursuing a Commercial Driver's License.

12. Additional Resources: We provided contact information, online resources, sample practice questions, and an index to support your learning and preparation.

Encouraging Safe Driving Habits

As you embark on your journey as a driver, we want to emphasize the importance of practicing safe driving habits. Always prioritize safety on the road, not only for your own well-being but also for the safety of others. Here are some key tips to remember:

- Stay Focused: Avoid distractions like texting or using your phone while driving. Keep your attention on the road.

- Obey Traffic Laws: Respect speed limits, traffic signals, and signs. Follow right-of-way rules and always yield to pedestrians.

- Drive Defensively: Anticipate the actions of other drivers and be prepared to react to potential hazards.

- Never Drive Impaired: Never get behind the wheel if you've consumed alcohol, drugs, or prescription medications that can impair your ability to drive safely.

- Practice Patience: Traffic congestion and delays can be frustrating, but patience is key to maintaining a calm and safe driving environment.

- Maintain Your Vehicle: Regularly check your vehicle's brakes, tires, lights, and other essential components to ensure it's in good working condition.

Best Wishes for Your Success

As you prepare for the Washington driving test, remember that knowledge, practice, and responsible behavior are your allies. Approach the test with confidence, knowing that you've equipped yourself with the skills and information needed to succeed.

We express our best wishes for your success on the Washington driving test and your future endeavors as a driver.

May you enjoy the freedom and responsibility that come with being a licensed driver while always prioritizing safety and responsibility on the road.

Safe travels, and may your journey be filled with many miles of safe and enjoyable driving experiences!

Appendix:

Your Handy Reference

In this appendix, we provide you with a glossary of terms to explain any technical or legal terminology used throughout the book. Additionally, we've included a selection of sample practice questions to help you test your knowledge and reinforce what you've learned. Use this valuable reference to clarify concepts and assess your readiness for the Washington driving test.

Glossary of Terms

1. Alcohol Concentration (BAC): The amount of alcohol in a person's bloodstream, measured as a percentage. In Washington, the legal limit for BAC while driving is 0.08%.

2. Blind Spot: An area around a vehicle that the driver cannot directly see through mirrors or peripheral vision.

3. Commercial Driver's License (CDL): A special driver's license is required to operate commercial vehicles, including trucks and buses.

4. Defensive Driving: A set of safe driving practices that help drivers anticipate and react to potential hazards on the road.

5. DMV (Department of Motor Vehicles): A government agency responsible for regulating driver licensing and vehicle registration.

6. DUI (Driving Under the Influence): The act of operating a vehicle while impaired by alcohol, drugs, or a combination of both.

7. Hazardous Materials (HazMat): Substances that, due to their nature, pose a risk to health, safety, or property during transportation.

8. Interstate Driving: Driving that involves crossing state lines.

9. Intrastate Driving: Driving that occurs entirely within one state's boundaries.

10. Lane Change: Moving from one lane to another while driving.

11. Learner's Permit: A provisional driver's license that allows new drivers to practice driving under certain restrictions.

12. Parallel Parking: Parking a vehicle parallel to the curb, often between two other parked vehicles.

13. Pedestrian: A person traveling on foot.

14. Right-of-Way: The legal right of one vehicle or pedestrian to proceed before another in a specific situation.

15. School Bus: A vehicle used to transport students to and from school, typically equipped with safety features.

16. Speed Limit: The maximum legal speed at which a vehicle can travel on a specific road or in a particular area.

17. Stop Sign: A red, octagonal sign that indicates drivers must come to a complete stop at an intersection.

18. Traffic Signal: A device that controls the flow of traffic at intersections, typically using red, yellow, and green lights.

19. Turn Signal: A signaling device on a vehicle that indicates the driver's intention to turn left or right.

20. Yield Sign: A red and white triangular sign that indicates drivers must yield the right-of-way.

Sample Practice Questions

Let's test your knowledge with these sample practice questions. Choose the correct answer for each question:

1. What does a yield sign mean?
   - A) Speed up and proceed through the intersection.
   - B) Come to a complete stop and wait for other traffic to clear.
   - C) Maintain your current speed and continue without stopping.
   - D) Sound your horn to alert other drivers.

Answer: B) Come to a complete stop and wait for other traffic to clear.

2. What is the legal limit for Blood Alcohol Concentration (BAC) while driving in Washington?
- A) 0.02%
- B) 0.04%
- C) 0.06%
- D) 0.08%

Answer: D) 0.08%

3. When approaching a school bus with flashing red lights and a stop sign extended, what should you do?
- A) Pass the bus if you're in a hurry.
- B) Slow down but proceed with caution.
- C) Stop and wait until the bus turns off its lights and retracts the stop sign.
- D) Honk your horn to alert the bus driver.

Answer: C) Stop and wait until the bus turns off its lights and retracts the stop sign.

4. What is a blind spot?
   - A) A section of the road where speed limits are enforced strictly.
   - B) An area around a vehicle that the driver cannot directly see through mirrors or peripheral vision.
   - C) A location where you can park your vehicle temporarily.
   - D) A designated area for pedestrian crossings.

Answer: B) An area around a vehicle that the driver cannot directly see through mirrors or peripheral vision.

5. What should you do if you encounter a steady yellow traffic signal?
   - A) Speed up and proceed through the intersection.

- B) Stop and wait for the light to turn green.
- C) Slow down and prepare to stop.
- D) Proceed with caution, but maintain your current speed.

Answer: C) Slow down and prepare to stop.

6. What is the purpose of defensive driving?
- A) To drive aggressively and assertively on the road.
- B) To anticipate and react to potential hazards on the road.
- C) To always maintain the maximum legal speed limit.
- D) To tailgate the vehicle in front to discourage other drivers from cutting in.

Answer: B) To anticipate and react to potential hazards on the road.

7. What is a learner's permit?
   - A) A type of driver's license for experienced drivers.
   - B) A provisional license for drivers aged 21 and older.
   - C) A temporary license for drivers under 18, allowing supervised driving.
   - D) A special license for driving large trucks and buses.

Answer: C) A temporary license for drivers under 18, allowing supervised driving.

8. What should you do when approaching a stop sign at an intersection?
   - A) Slow down but proceed without stopping.
   - B) Come to a complete stop, yield to other vehicles, and proceed when safe.
   - C) Speed up to clear the intersection quickly.

- D) Honk your horn to alert other drivers.

Answer: B) Come to a complete stop, yield to other vehicles, and proceed when safe.

9. What does a red and white triangular sign with an exclamation point mean?
   - A) Yield ahead.
   - B) Caution: Slow down and be prepared to stop.
   - C) No passing zone.
   - D) Speed limit reduction zone.

Answer: B) Caution: Slow down and be prepared to stop.

10. What is the legal age for obtaining a Commercial Driver's License (CDL) for interstate driving in Washington?
    - A) 18 years old.
    - B) 19 years old.
    - C) 20 years old.
    - D) 21 years old.

Answer: D) 21 years old.

Feel free to review these practice questions as often as needed to reinforce your understanding of the concepts covered in this book. Keep studying, stay safe on the road, and best of luck on your Washington driving test!